Becoming Mine

Letters From the Woman I Became

Lueella Shelton

Shelton Legacy Press, LLC

COPYRIGHT © 2025 BY Shelton Legacy Press, LLC

Shelton Legacy Press, LLC
PO Box 529
Cedar Creek, TX 78612

All rights reserved. No part of this publication may be reproduced, stored in a retrieval system, or transmitted in any form or by any means—electronic, mechanical, photocopying, recording, or otherwise—without the prior written permission of the author, except in the case of brief quotations used in critical articles or reviews. Exceptions are permitted under Section 107 or 108 of the 1976 United States Copyright Act.

Library of Congress Cataloging-in-Publication Data

Identifiers: Library of Congress Control Number: 2025916647

Name: Lueella Shelton, 2025-author.
Title: Becoming Mine: Letters From the Woman I Became
Book Three of the Series tilted: Ink to Paper: A Love in Three Seasons

ISBN: 979-8-9997335-4-2 (Paperback), 979-8-9997335-5-9 (Hardback), 979-8-9997335-8-0 (Kindle)

Printed in the United States of America

To you—

The one who stirred the words from silence.
The one who turned touch into scripture.
The one who made my heart brave enough to write.

These poems were born because of you—
because loving you demanded language I didn't yet have.
Because even in absence, your name stayed soft on my tongue.

This book is not just a record of what we shared.
It is a record of what love became—
when it deepened, when it quieted, when it endured.
When it hurt. When it healed.
When it held me still.

Every line I wrote was a reaching.
Every pause, a prayer.
Every page, proof that devotion doesn't always ask for forever—only for truth.

You are in every word.
And I wouldn't change a single one.

—L.S.

Acknowledgements

To write is to live twice—once in the moment, and again in the telling. This book, and the entire *Ink to Paper* trilogy, exists because of the people who have walked with me through both.

To my family—thank you for loving me without condition and for giving me roots deep enough to grow in any direction. Your support has been my anchor, your faith my steady compass.

To my friends, who have cheered for me in both the bright days and the shadowed ones—you've held space for my words, my silences, and my becoming. Thank you for showing up, for listening, and for reminding me that vulnerability is not weakness but strength.

To the man who inspired these poems—your presence in my life has been both the muse and the mirror. Through you, I have learned more about love, resilience, and myself than I ever thought possible. Thank you for the moments that sparked my pen, for the peace you've offered, and for the lessons that live between the lines.

To my readers—you are the reason these pages leave my hands and find their way into the world. Thank you for opening your hearts to my story and for finding pieces of your own within it. You've proven that poetry is not just about the writer—it's a shared space, a conversation, a place where lives meet on the page.

And to God—the ultimate Author—thank You for every chapter, every detour, and every return. Thank You for the courage to tell my truth and the wisdom to know that every season, every line, is part of Your greater narrative.

This is not goodbye. There are more poems, more seasons, more truths still to come. But for now, I thank you—from the depth of my heart—for being part of this one.

—Lueella Shelton

Poetic Invocation

Come,
sit with me in this softer light.
The storm has passed,
the air still carries the scent of rain,
and I have learned the beauty of breathing
without the ache in my chest.

I will not tell you how to heal.
I will only tell you how I found my way—
how I traced the map back to myself
one small truth at a time.

These pages are not a goodbye.
They are an opening.
A return.
A hand extended—
not to pull you forward,
but to walk beside you
as you arrive where you already belong.

Preface

When I began this trilogy, I thought I was telling the story of a love. In truth, I was telling the story of a woman—
the woman I was, the woman I became, and the woman I am still becoming.

The Spark and the Surrender was the beginning—
the wild rush of being seen and chosen,
the unguarded joy of falling.

The Silence Between was the middle—
the space where longing and questions grew louder,
where love became a quiet weight in my hands.

And now, Becoming Mine—
the place where I stop looking for clarity in someone else's eyes
and begin to find it in my own reflection.

This is not the story of walking away bitter.
It is the story of standing in peace.
It is not the closing of a door,
but the opening of one inward.

Every poem here is a letter—
some to the man who sparked these words,
some to the girl who needed to hear them,
and most of all, to the woman who finally listened.

If you have ever lost yourself in loving,
and found yourself in letting go—
you will recognize this journey.
And I hope, somewhere in these lines,
you find your own hand waiting for you to take it.

—Lueella Shelton

Table of Content

Acknowledgements..ii
Poetic Invocation..iv
Preface...v

Section One

Where the Healing Started...2
Letter to the Reader: "Where Peace Resides"......................4
    Where Peace Resides 6
Letter to the Reader: "The Shape of My Thanks"...............9
    The Shape of My Thanks 11
Letter to the Reader: "Just As You Are"............................13
    Just As You Are 14
Letter to the Reader: "Let Love Be the Foundation".........17
    Let Love Be the Foundation 18

Section Two

Not Just Surviving..20
Letter to the Reader: "He's Home"....................................22
    He's Home..24
Letter to the Reader: "Where He Dreamed"......................28
    Where He Dreamed..30
Letter to the Reader: "And It Is Good".............................32
    And It Is Good...34
Letter to the Reader: "Wrapped in Your Arms, I Rise"......36
    Wrapped in Your Arms, I Rise 38

Section Three

Whole, Even Still..44
Letter to the Reader: "You Rise for Me"..........................46
    You Rise for Me 48
Letter to the Reader: "I Am Not Your Secret"...............50
    I Am Not Your Secret..51
Letter to the Reader: "It Is Well With My Soul"............54
    It Is Well With My Soul 55

Section Four

Home Is My Own Name...58
Letter to the Reader: "Becoming Mine"..........................60
    Becoming Mine..62
Letter to the Reader: "The Love of Her Own Life".......65
    The Love of Her Own Life..67

Closing Letter to the Reader

Dear Reader..70
    Benediciton..73
Epilogue..74
About the Author...76

SECTION ONE

Where the Healing Started

The turning point—choosing peace, releasing weight, and honoring the self as worthy.

Before there was peace, there was unraveling.
Before the quiet, there was a storm so loud I forgot what stillness felt like.

This section holds the first steps back—
the tender, trembling moments when I began to choose myself without turning away from love. Here, the wounds were still fresh, but my hands had stopped pressing on them. I had learned to let them breathe.

Healing didn't arrive like a miracle.
It came slowly—
in mornings where the air felt softer,
in conversations that didn't end in exhaustion,
in the way I started to see my own reflection without flinching.

These poems mark the shift.
The moment I understood that love could remain even when I was no longer willing to harm myself to keep it. That I could hold someone in my heart while also holding space for my own becoming.

Here, the foundation of my healing began—
built not on forgetting the hurt, but on choosing to live beyond it.
This is where I learned that the heart can still be tender after breaking, and that love, when it is true, will not stand in the way of your wholeness.

These are the pages where the woman I was
began to make peace with the woman I was becoming.

—L.S.

Letter to the Reader: "Where Peace Resides"

This poem was born in the still of a quiet morning—one of those sacred hours where the world hasn't quite woken up and your thoughts rise like soft steam from a cup of tea.

That morning, I found myself reflecting on the subtle yet powerful transformation that happens when healing takes root. When you've lived long enough in chaos, dysfunction can feel like home. But when peace enters—authentically, consistently—you begin to taste what true wellness feels like. You realize just how intolerable that old noise has become. You stop seeking fires to put out and start protecting your calm like sacred ground.

I wrote a message to the man I love—my safe place. I wanted him to know that the peace I've come to cherish, and the clarity I now claim, is largely because of his presence in my life. His calm. His gentleness. His honesty. His unwavering support. Through him, I've learned how to sit still in my own soul. I've learned that healing doesn't just happen alone—it happens when someone stands beside you and reminds you of who you are, even when you forget.

His response humbled me. With quiet strength, he reminded me that he doesn't see himself as the source, only the mirror reflecting what was already in me. That he's far from perfect, still learning, still growing. But he promised to remain—simple, supportive, loving—as long as I'd allow him to.

"Where Peace Resides" is about that sacred exchange. It's about the gift of becoming whole in someone's presence—not because they fix you, but because they never force you to break again. It's about the kind of love that doesn't stir chaos, but cultivates calm. The kind that says, "I see you becoming," and simply stays to witness it all.

If you've ever found that kind of peace in another—or within yourself—this poem is for you.

With love and gratitude,

–L.S.

Where Peace Resides

There comes a time
when the soul remembers
what healing feels like—
when the body, once broken,
learns the difference
between surviving and being whole.

Chaos,
once tolerated like stale air,
is now a foreign storm
I can no longer breathe in.
Stress tastes like fast food—
once devoured without question,
now rejected
by a spirit reawakened.

Yesterday's noise tried to return—
early, heavy, relentless.
But today...
today arrived quiet.
Soft.
Still.
Even the house rests in reverence
to this morning's calm.

And I know—
I know this peace
has your fingerprints.

You,
the quiet strength
who poured into me

when I didn't know I was thirsty.
You,
the mirror that showed me
my reflection in the light,
not the dark.

Because of you,
I rise rooted.
Because of you,
my esteem grows in soil you helped till.
Because of you,
I know now how to name the peace
when it visits.

And still you say—
I take little credit.
Still you speak
with the humility of a man
who knows storms
but refuses to drown in them.

You say,
I will continue to love and support you
for as long as you will have me.

So stay, Love.
Stay for the quiet mornings
and shared sunshine,
for the joy you give
without demand.
You are no burden—
you are blessing.

In your calm,
I found clarity.
In your love,
I found the truth of myself.

Together,
we bloom.

Letter to the Reader: "The Shape of My Thanks"

There are moments when "thank you" feels too small—too plain—to carry the depth of what the heart truly feels. *The Shape of My Thanks* was born in one of those moments. A quiet evening, a full heart, and the realization that the language of gratitude is more than polite words—it's a lived emotion, a sacred offering, a mirror held up to love.

The original poem, titled *Gratitude*, was written as a personal letter to the man who has consistently shown up for me—not just in grand gestures, but in everyday ways that whisper, "You matter." I wrote it when my spoken words failed me, when what I felt was far too wide for speech and needed the soft unfolding of a pen across paper.

In him, I found something I had longed for without knowing: not perfection, but presence. A steady warmth. A soul that glows like the moon—always showing up in the dark to remind me that light still exists. That I am not alone.

This poem is my attempt to give form—shape—to that feeling. It is the embodiment of my thanks: curved in longing, grounded in admiration, and overflowing with the desire to know him wholly, deeply, beyond just the surface.

It is not merely an ode to romantic love. It's a celebration of those who come into our lives and stay. Who listen between the lines. Who become our soft place, our safe place, our home. *The Shape of My Thanks* is for anyone who has ever been transformed by the simple, powerful act of being truly seen and gently held.

So, if you've ever loved someone so deeply that ordinary gratitude felt like an understatement, this poem is for you.

With love,

—L.S.

The Shape of My Thanks

I am without the language for speaking
yet overflowing with the words that write themselves—
pouring freely from the quiet center of me.

Words that sketch the silhouette of a man—
so beautiful,
so rare,
so wholly you.

I am grateful for you—
not in part,
but in the whole of your being.

You are as perfect as the moon—
a constant light.
You shine across my chaos,
casting peace where there once was ache.
Your glow turns my darkness
into a sacred kind of joy.

This gratitude I carry—
there is no scale to hold it.
I doubt even the ruler
knows the measure of what I feel.

But this I know for sure:
I love you.
Fully.
Exactly as you are.

You are special.
You matter.

You move the pieces of my world
in quiet, extraordinary ways.

I crave more than flesh.
I crave your voice—
your thoughts,
your roots,
your dreams,
and even your fears.

I don't just want to taste your skin,
I want to know you in full—
unmasked, unfiltered, unafraid.

Just you.
As you are.

All my better days
are the ones touched by your presence.
And for that—
I am endlessly,
wordlessly,
gratefully yours.

Letter to the Reader: "Just As You Are"

There are some people whose presence alone settles the soul. They don't have to arrive with fanfare or fix the broken things. They simply exist in your world—steady, present, and kind—and somehow, that changes everything. *Just As You Are* is a love letter to such a person.

This poem came from a moment of stillness—after the dishes were cleared, the air still carrying the quiet joy of Thanksgiving. I found myself reflecting not just on the day, but on the man who joined me in it. A man who doesn't demand a performance or perfection, but meets me in every space with calm, consistency, and care.

When spoken words felt insufficient, the pen made room for what my heart couldn't contain. I wrote to honor him—not just for what he does, but for who he is. His gestures, both grand and simple—a bottle of wine, a warm bowl of soup, a thoughtful ride—each one a quiet echo of his devotion.

Just As You Are is a tribute to the kind of love that doesn't ask you to change or perform. It celebrates presence over performance, soul over surface. It craves depth, not just touch. It honors the kind of connection that reaches beyond attraction and into alignment.

If you've ever had the honor of loving or being loved by someone who brings you peace, who helps your world feel a little less chaotic and a little more whole—this poem is for you. It's my reminder, and now perhaps yours, that love—real love—doesn't need fixing, only recognizing.

With gratitude,

–L.S.

Just As You Are

inspired by a letter dated 11/26

I am without the language
to speak it out loud—
but my heart knows how to write.

Words pour freely from within me,
painting the shape
of a man
so beautiful,
so exceptional,
so completely you.

I am grateful—
for the whole of you,
not in part,
but in your fullness.

You are as perfect as the moon,
a steady light
shining through my distress,
casting peace on the shadows
I once called home.

Your light
turns my darkness
into something joyful—
bright,
soft,
safe.

This gratitude I hold for you
cannot be measured.
Even the ruler
does not know its own rules.

But this I know for sure:
I love you.
Fully.
Freely.
Just as you are.

You are special.
You matter.
You make life feel
more possible.

And I crave—
not just the heat of your skin,
but the warmth of your thoughts.
I want your words,
your depths,
your quiet longings,
your hidden fears.

I want to know
where you came from
and what you still hope to become.

I yearn—
not only to taste you,
but to know you,
beneath the surface,
beyond the physical,
into the sacred.

All my better days
have you in them.

Like Thanksgiving—
your soup,
your wine,
your hands on the wheel
when I needed to be carried.

You are always the calm to my storm.
You make the road easier.
You make the noise quieter.
You make life feel peaceful.

And I love it.
I delight in it.
I delight in you.

Letter to the Reader: "Let Love Be the Foundation"

At the core of every enduring relationship—whether romantic, platonic, or familial—there must be something deeper than fleeting emotion or momentary pleasure. There must be truth. There must be care. There must be a love that does not delight in harm, but instead seeks to heal.

Let Love Be the Foundation was born in a moment of reconciliation, reflection, and sincere longing for what's right over what's easy. The original piece, simply titled *Love*, was more than just a declaration; it was a plea. A soft yet firm reminder that in the midst of missteps, miscommunication, or even silence—love, true love, must remain.

This poem does not romanticize perfection. It honors imperfection with humility. It acknowledges pain, but chooses not to stay there. Instead, it chooses to build—a life, a bond, a future—on something honest, patient, and enduring.

If you've ever loved someone deeply, you know that love isn't just a feeling—it's a decision. A daily recommitment to see the best, speak the truth, and return to grace when things go wrong. That is what this poem hopes to leave with you.

Let it remind you that when everything else falters, you can still choose love. You can still build from that place.

With open-hearted sincerity,

—L.S.

Let Love Be the Foundation

formerly titled "Love"

Love takes no pleasure in harm—
it rejoices in the truth.

And the truth is:
I love you.
I find no peace
in anything that breaks us.

When all else falters...
when words fail,
when wounds linger—
love remains.

So let's build from there.
Let's build on love.

SECTION TWO

Not Just Surviving

Beyond recovery, the speaker begins to thrive—finding joy, presence, and intimacy, that nurtures rather than drains.

There was a time when I thought survival was enough.
When breathing through the day without breaking felt like victory.
When I wore my endurance like a medal, never realizing it was also a weight.

But surviving is not the same as living.
And living—truly living—requires more than making it to tomorrow.

This section marks the turning point.
The moment I stopped counting the days I'd endured
and began creating days I wanted to remember.
It's where I learned that love could be more than a life raft—
it could be a home, a garden, a place where joy could grow without apology.

The poems here are not about avoiding pain.
They are about refusing to let pain be the whole story.
They speak to the mornings I woke without dread,
the nights that ended in laughter instead of silence,
the moments I felt not just safe, but seen.

This is where the pace of my heart began to match the pace of my hope.
Where I discovered that wholeness is not found by looking backward,
but by choosing—again and again—to live fully in the now.

In these pages, you will not just find survival.
You will find the proof that I began to thrive.

Survival kept me breathing.
    Love taught me how to live.

–L.S.

Letter to the Reader: "He's Home"

"He's Home" was born from a quiet evening layered with anticipation, relief, and the deep, wordless comfort that love often brings after distance. The poem reflects a single day—one that began with ordinary chaos and ended in extraordinary peace. It was written from a June journal entry in which life's small decisions—keys exchanged, meals prepared, phone calls made—wove themselves into something sacred: the moment of his return.

When I wrote that entry, my day had been full—work, errands, laughter over lunch with a dear friend. Yet beneath it all, there was this gentle hum of expectancy. He had been away, and though I am an independent woman who moves confidently through her days, I've come to realize that home isn't a fixed address for me—it's a presence. It's *him*.

The poem captures that shift from routine to revelation. It is the smell of his cigar drifting in through the rain, the sight of smoke before the sight of him, and the sudden thrum of joy that rises when love announces itself without a word. That familiar scent became the signal: *he's home*.

In our story, there is no grand arrival—no fireworks, no declarations. Just small gestures filled with meaning: a meal simmering on the stove, a kiss to the neck, a shared chair, a quiet gift exchanged. The beauty lies in the simplicity of care and in the knowing that true partnership does not need spectacle to feel profound.

"He's Home" is a celebration of rhythm—the rhythm of two lives finding comfort in each other after long days apart. It's about the peace that comes when a lover returns, when you no longer have to measure the distance between breaths, and when the ordinary becomes extraordinary because you are together again.

This poem is also, in part, a love letter to the kind of man who moves with intention. The one who doesn't need to announce his devotion because it's visible in how he listens, how he enters a room, how he quietly creates safety and steadiness.

As you read *He's Home,* I hope you feel the intimacy of a slow evening—the rain outside, the smell of something familiar, the simple holiness of being seen, known, and loved.

With warmth,

–L.S.

He's Home

This morning started in motion—
keys shuffled between plans,
doors, and gas compartments,
a dance of logistics and waiting.
He called—my guy—
with updates wrapped in intention.
Midnight, he said.
Not yet.
Hold the key.
Keep it close.

Work called,
then laughter over lunch with Mo,
two women smiling wide
about the men who have surprised us
with care, with comfort,
with the thrill of something new
and right now.

I gathered things for his return.
Home came later than planned—
but no rush,
just oxtails on the stove
and my pen in hand.

Then a call—no, my call—
to tell him I'd arrived.
A habit we'd never formed
because he is always with me
or coming behind me.

But tonight,
he was ahead of me.

The bad news:
he turned down a job.
The good news:
he was already on the road,
headed home—
to me.
Not at 3 a.m.,
but by seven.
My soul leapt.

We spoke until music took over.
He needed his quiet
to think, to ride.
I returned to cooking,
to writing,
to the storm's hush
just outside the door.

And then—
that smell.
His cigar.
So familiar
it made my heart run
before my feet did.
I looked—once, twice—
until smoke proved he was near.

He had watched me
before I even knew.
He kissed my neck,
and all of me exhaled:
He's home.

He took his time,
brought his things in,

settled gently—
and I gave him space
because that's what love does.
I finished writing,
finished dinner,
showered,
and made room for him
like always.

He sat,
I joined.
He opened the gift,
read my letter,
kissed me softly,
thanked me.

Later,
he rocked me
to sleep with nothing but his body,
his rhythm,
his knowing of me.

He asked,
You okay?
And I said,
Of course. I have you.
That's all there is.

He is worthy—
of every soft thing
I can give,
of every untouched piece
I once guarded.

And I—
I love him,
without barter,
without fear,

with joy,
with ease.

He's home.
And so am I.

Letter to the Reader: "Where He Dreamed"

"Where He Dreamed" captures an intimate, sacred moment between two people whose connection has matured beyond mere desire—it lives in rhythm, trust, and unspoken knowing. The poem was drawn directly from a journal entry written in the stillness of early morning, when love felt both tender and timeless.

That morning unfolded quietly—before the first hint of daylight, before the world began its daily hum. In that hushed space, love revealed itself not through words, but through touch. What I sought to preserve in this poem was not only the sensuality of the encounter, but also the spiritual intimacy that comes from being fully known by another human being.

It is easy to read "Where He Dreamed" and see only passion. But look deeper, and you'll find communion—two souls moving in harmony, mirroring one another's pace, breath, and release. His hands traced a familiar map, not to conquer or claim, but to remember—to honor every curve, every story written in flesh. In that moment, our bodies were not separate instruments but a single melody, rising toward dawn.

The title itself speaks to intention. It refers not just to physical arrival, but to emotional alignment—to reaching the place he had long dreamed of, where love is mutual and anchored in both tenderness and trust. The kiss at the end of the poem is more than closure; it is reverence. It says, *I see you. I thank you. I honor this.*

This piece, like much of my work, is an honest reflection of love as lived, not imagined. It acknowledges that intimacy is not simply an act—it's an exchange of truth, a language without words, where safety allows vulnerability to flourish.

As you read "Where He Dreamed," I invite you to look beyond the physical and into the quiet holiness of connection—the way love can slow time, silence fear, and make the sunrise feel like a continuation of a prayer whispered between two souls.

With tenderness,

–L.S.

Where He Dreamed

In the hush before the sun,
when morning is still a secret
and shadows wrap the room in reverence,
he turns—
quiet as breath—
into a spoon
and gathers me in.

His arms,
a harbor.
His body,
a promise pressed against my back.
He holds me—
snug, certain,
as if the night were never meant to end.

Fingers trace me slowly,
a deliberate reverence,
finding my breast,
awakening its ache.
He plays the rhythm of want
on the tip of my nipple
until I hum beneath his hands.

His touch travels—
down my hips,
over my thigh,
up the slope of my back,
across the curve of my shoulder,
through my tangled hair—

a cartographer
mapping terrain
he knows by memory
yet explores like new land.

Then the shift—
the flip—
his knees part me
like the opening of day.
I unfold beneath him,
blooming into the space he's made.

We move—
together,
rising on the tide
we create with our rhythm.
No words—
just gasps,
moans,
a breath held
then released
in perfect unison.

And when we arrive—
together,
shaking with something deeper than heat—
he kisses me
soft,
sure,
sacred,
as if sealing the moment
he had dreamed of
all night.

Letter to the Reader: "And It Is Good"

The poem *"And It Is Good"* was born out of a moment of still reflection—a moment when love, desire, and faith intertwined so seamlessly that I could no longer separate one from the other. It was written in June of 2022, during a time when I was learning to embrace the fullness of human connection without guilt or reservation, recognizing that even passion, when rooted in genuine love, is divine.

This poem celebrates the sensory experience of loving someone completely. It acknowledges that intimacy is not only physical—it is spiritual, emotional, and deeply sacred. In writing it, I wanted to honor the way love manifests through the senses: how we *see*, *touch*, *taste*, *hear*, and *smell* the presence of the one who moves us. Every sensation, every moment shared, becomes an act of worship in its own right.

The phrase "and it is good" comes from the language of creation itself. In Genesis, after each act of creation, God declares His work good. That repetition always struck me—not as divine pride, but as divine recognition. A reminder that what is made from love, and experienced through love, carries holiness within it. When I wrote, *"I smell him and it is good. I taste him and it is good…"* I was not just describing passion; I was naming a sacred truth—*that love, when pure and mutual, is inherently good.*

Through this poem, I wanted to dissolve the boundaries between sensual and spiritual love. Too often, women—especially women of faith—are told that the body is separate from the spirit, that desire exists outside of holiness. Yet what I have come to know through lived experience is that when love is expressed freely, without harm or shame, it becomes a mirror of God's own creation—intentional, tender, and whole.

"And It Is Good" is a testimony to that knowing. It is a hymn to embodied love, to the kind of intimacy that slows time and softens fear, reminding us that joy can be sacred, and pleasure can be prayer.

As you read this poem, I hope you will feel not just the warmth of romance, but the reverence of it—the awareness that to love and be loved so completely is, in itself, an act of grace.

With all my senses awake,

–L.S.

And It Is Good

His fragrance—
A rich exuberance,
Lingers in the air
Like a whispered promise.
His taste—
An indulgence beyond restraint,
A luxury of self
That I savor
Again and again.

His touch—
So gentle,
Yet electric—
Floods my body
With waves of oxytocin,
Desire dancing
Along serotonin's path,
Arousing every inch of me
In ways only he can.

Every moment—
Etched in memory,
Imprinted on the walls
Of my mind.
There is not a day
He doesn't reshape
My heart's architecture.

All things made by God,
God said: It is good.

And he—
He is oh so good.

All my senses
Sing of him.
I smell him—
And it is good.
I taste him—
And it is good.
I touch him—
And it is good.
I hear him—
And it is good.
I see him—
And it is good.

He is goodness
Wrapped in skin,
A blessing too bold
For ordinary time.

With him,
The hours disappear—
Held in his arms,
Bound by his charm,
Every second is divine.

But when he leaves,
Time takes its revenge.
The days stretch,
The clock resumes.
And I—
I linger
In the longing,
Waiting for time
To pause again
In his presence.

Letter to the Reader: "Wrapped in Your Arms, I Rise"

Some poems are born from beauty. Others from heartbreak. But this one—*Wrapped in Your Arms, I Rise*—was born from both. It came from a space I once held sacred, a space filled with warmth, vulnerability, and unflinching truth. A space where love lived even when certainty didn't.

The original letter this poem draws from was not written for performance or poetic praise. It was written from one heart to another—raw, unscripted, and aching with a complicated kind of love. In it, I wrestled with the paradox of being wrapped in someone's arms while also carrying the weight of knowing those arms might one day hold someone else.

Love is often painted as soft and simple, but this poem explores the complexity of what it means to love someone who hasn't yet decided if they can love you back the same way. Not out of cruelty, but out of damage. Out of wounds too deep to name. And still, you stay— not out of weakness, but because *when you are with them, you rise.*

The poem is not a plea. It is not a protest. It is a declaration of the way love—when real—refuses to be silenced by disappointment or dulled by time. It chooses to see the whole person, flaws and all. And still it says: *I will not let go, not because I am blind, but because I see you fully—and you are still worth it.*

For anyone who's ever given their whole heart and stood still in the ache of loving someone who is still healing—this poem is for you. For anyone who's known the calm of another's arms while storm clouds brewed above—this poem is for you. And for anyone who has learned to love themselves better through loving another, *this poem is you.*

With courage and grace,

–L.S.

Wrapped in Your Arms, I Rise

—a poem drawn from a love letter

You are loved.
And I love you—
not because it sounds good,
but because it is truth.

A truth
you haven't heard enough,
one you still hesitate to believe.
You, who think love is earned
or lost in your mistakes—
forgetting that love
was always a gift from God,
distorted by the wounds of men.

You are loved
as someone's son,
brother,
father,
friend.
But I love the whole of you—
the good, the bad,
the flawed and beautiful mess
that makes you you.

You are imperfect—
so am I.
But you, My Love,
are perfect for me.
And with my love

comes room to falter
and the promise that I will stay
when you do.

There is much we carry,
much we must unlearn.
We aged.
We ache.
We choose who we want to become.
And you made it clear—
November 22,
in the year of our divorces—
that no woman stood a chance
after the last one.

So I remained quiet,
embracing the space you gave me,
even as it hurt to be kept at a distance.

Still, I promised two things:
to love you as you are—
and to never lie to you.
I have kept both.
My life is transparent,
offered to you wholly,
even when the truths were
uncomfortable to bear.

Wrapped in your arms,
I found strength.
Wrapped in your arms,
I began to heal.
Wrapped in your arms,
I felt safe.
Even when we were still
bound to others by law,
you were peace in my chaos—
water to my fire,

gentle, strong,
a feather pressed against my skin.

You are amazing,
and I meant it—
on the ship,
in the silence,
and when I said,
"She can have you."

I said it not from strength
but from emptiness—
from feeling unwanted,
unseen.
And when you pulled away
in November's cold,
my world collapsed.

And still...
we found our way back.
We always do.

You said "I love you"
for the first time—
in all caps.
I didn't answer.
Not out of cruelty,
but confusion.
Why now?
What had changed?

We resumed our greetings,
but the space between them
remained quiet.
Then came July 12th.
You wrote,
"I love and miss you. Good night."

And I paused,
because something in me shifted.

I came down to listen—
not to argue,
not to plead.
I needed to hear the why in your love.
Not because I doubt,
but because love,
real love,
asks for clarity, not perfection.

That day, I chose you again—
knowing we were in something
we never meant to build.
And I returned
with a full heart,
ready to be with you,
not just near you.

But even now,
she lingers—
in shadows,
in messages,
in emojis I don't understand,
but know enough to delete.

I will not fight for what
has made it clear
it isn't worth fighting for.
I will not ask,
"Am I enough?"
or "What does she have that I lack?"
Because I already know—
this isn't about her.
This has always been about you.

And still,
I do not ask.
I do not seek answers
where peace already lives.
I will not bite bait
meant to wound.
And this—this—is the last I'll say of her.

You are loved.
Wholly.
Still.
Always.

What I see in you
has always outweighed
what others may not.
You are greater than your demons.
Stronger than your flaws.
You are My Love.
And I will stay
for as long as you choose
to have me near.

I told you once,
and I'll tell you again—
I will not let you go.
Because you are simply
too wonderful to release.
You are
exceptionally phenomenal—
indeed.

SECTION THREE

Whole, Even Still

Love continues to echo, but the speaker stands whole with or without it—secure in her own worth.

By the time we arrive here, the story has shifted.

The wounds have closed, but the scars remain—reminders of where I've been, not weights to carry. The ache no longer demands center stage.

This section is about what comes after the hardest parts are faced, when love is no longer something to survive and healing is no longer a question of if, but how. Here, I have learned that I am not defined by what I've lost or even by what I've kept. I am whole—not because life has been flawless, but because I've chosen to stand in my own truth regardless.

These are the poems that hold the quiet proof:
that peace can exist alongside uncertainty,
that love can last without erasing the self,
and that joy can grow again in soil once thought barren.

In these pages, I no longer look for permission to claim my space in love and in life. I have learned that my wholeness is not conditional—it is mine, even still.

If the earlier sections were about healing and learning to live again, this one is about living fully. It is about carrying both tenderness and strength without apology. It is about loving and being loved with open hands, trusting that what is meant for me will meet me without force.

This is the place where I no longer question my worth.
Where I can look at myself—heart, history, and all—and say:
Yes. I am whole. Even still.

> "I have been broken.
> I have been healed.
> And still—I am whole."

—L.S.

Letter to the Reader: "You Rise for Me"

"You Rise for Me" is a love letter to constancy.

There are few things more sacred in love than knowing someone shows up for you—consistently, quietly, and without needing to be asked. *You Rise for Me* is a poem born from the gentle power of that knowing. It is a thank you that found its rhythm in a single, ordinary moment, when I paused long enough to realize how extraordinary it is to be loved by someone dependable.

The letter that gave life to this poem was never intended for public eyes. It was a note—a small offering—to the one who shows up for me the way the sun does: unwavering and full of quiet brilliance. It wasn't about grand gestures or romantic declarations, but about the quiet reassurances that show up in everyday love. The kind of love that doesn't need to announce itself, because its presence is felt like the turning of the earth beneath your feet.

In this poem, "rising" becomes a metaphor for presence—for being the one who stands with you when life grows heavy. It's about that person who makes it a little easier to breathe, simply because they're there. It's also a reminder that strength in love isn't always loud or dramatic. Sometimes, it's as soft as the morning sun and just as essential.

This poem is for anyone who's ever had someone who showed up—steadily, reliably, and with quiet devotion. And it's also for those who *are* that person for someone else. Because to rise for another, over and over again, is one of the most loving things we can ever do.

May you recognize the ones who rise for you. May you rise for them in return.

With gratitude,

—L.S.

You Rise for Me

inspired by a letter dated 12/7/22

Have I ever told you
how reassuring it is
to have you in my corner?
Not loud,
not boastful—
just there.
Just steady.

You are like the sun—
I do not wonder
if you'll appear.
I know you will.
You rise
without needing to be asked.
You rise
even when clouds make it hard to see.

And that—
that is the quiet miracle
of being loved by you.

I can do anything,
because you believe.
Because you show up.
Because you stand still
when everything else moves.

Thank you
for rising with me,
for rising for me—

not once,
but always.

You are loved.
So deeply.
And I love you—
not just for what you do,
but for who you continue to be
each time the light returns.

Letter to the Reader: "I Am Not Your Secret"

This poem was born from a moment of deep clarity and unflinching self-worth. *I Am Not Your Secret* is more than a declaration of love—it is a bold affirmation of dignity, desire, and the refusal to remain hidden in a space meant to be sacred and seen.

The original letter was written in the quiet between two truths: the love I feel and the love I deserve. In it, I poured out the ache and beauty of loving someone deeply, yet privately. There comes a time in every woman's life when silence is no longer peace, and privacy begins to feel like erasure. I wrote from that threshold, where love must either come into the light or lose its way in the shadows.

This is not a letter asking for grand displays. It is not a demand for tradition or performance. Instead, it is a truth spoken plainly: *I am worthy of being known. I am not a secret.*

The poem that grew from that truth is for every woman who has ever whispered her value into the darkness, hoping it would echo back in recognition. It is for those who have loved with fierce loyalty and clarity, and who are now learning to expect love that stands tall—out loud and unashamed.

To love someone is to elevate them. But to love *yourself* is to know when elevation must be mutual. You are not someone to be hidden. You are not a half-truth or an asterisk. You are the whole story—and you deserve to be read aloud.

With unshakable love and light,

—L.S.

I Am Not Your Secret

inspired by a letter of love, truth, and claiming

Everybody needs somebody
to lean on.
And I—
I found a king.

Not in a palace,
but in presence.
Not in wealth,
but in wisdom.

A man with a humble heart,
whose strength does not shout,
but steadies.

Everything I've spoken of you
has been truth.
Every word,
a confirmation
of what I already knew—
that you are a king
worthy of being known,
not hidden.

And I?
I no longer wish
to be treated like a queen.
I want to be the queen—
your queen.
The only one who reigns beside you.

Not in ritual,
but in realness.

I'm not asking for a ceremony
or a house key.
I'm not begging for rings
or titles.
I'm telling you—
I know who I am.

I know what I offer.
I know what I desire.
And I desire a man
who chooses to be kept.
Not scattered.
Not borrowed.
Not bound to secrecy.

I became your wife
in the eyes of God
the day I gave you my body
and my trust.

And now,
I can no longer remain
the hidden truth
in your story.

I want the world to know
the man who brings me joy.
The man who sees me,
hears me,
holds me.

When we began,
we spoke with honesty—
about broken vows
and silent departures.

We both knew
this would lead somewhere.

And now,
here we are.

So if I am your queen,
then let it be known—
not in shadows,
but in light.
Not in silence,
but in truth.

Because love—
real love—
deserves to be seen.

Letter to the Reader: "It Is Well With My Soul"

The poem *It Is Well With My Soul* was born from a moment of deep reflection—one that often comes after attending a funeral. There, in the presence of loss, we are given the rare opportunity to look inward. The ritual of saying goodbye to someone we love invites us not only to mourn the life that has passed, but also to honor the lives that remain. We begin to realize how fleeting time is, how sacred connection becomes, and how urgent it is to speak love while it can still be heard.

This poem is not only an ode to grief, but a celebration of life and love as it exists in the present. It is a tribute to a man who, in the ordinary rhythm of our lives, showed up as something extraordinary. A friend, a lover, a safe space. In him, I saw royalty—not in title, but in tenderness, in grace, and in his presence.

There is a quiet kind of surrender in truly loving someone. It's not dramatic or performative. It's a soul's yielding—a deep-seated knowing that says, *"You matter to me in ways words may never fully express."* The line *"To you my soul will yield, and it is well with my soul"* is my attempt to name that knowing. It's a declaration of peace, even in the midst of life's unpredictability.

I hope that as you read this piece, you feel reminded to reach for those you love. To celebrate them now. To speak your gratitude without hesitation. And to embrace the truth that when love is real, even in silence, it remains well with the soul.

With peace,

—L.S.

It Is Well With My Soul

A funeral grants us pause—
to honor the one we've lost,
yes,
but also to cherish
those who still walk among us,
breathing,
beating,
becoming.

You,
my dear sweet friend,
are one such soul—
an exceptional man,
a quiet King
mighty in your own right,
crowned not by ceremony
but by the way you live,
give,
remain.

Your life is worth celebrating
now,
while you are still here
to feel it.

Know this:
I value you in full,
as you are,
not for what you offer
but for who you are.

I love you—
far deeper than you'll ever believe.
You have been a gift
to the days I've lived.
And for this,
my soul will yield.
And it is well—
with my soul,
because of you.

You are loved.
And I love you.
Always.

SECTION FOUR

Home Is My Own Name

The final arrival—choosing self as the truest home, with love offered freely but never at the cost of identity.

By the time we reach this final section, the search has ended.
Not because the questions disappeared,
but because I no longer need someone else's answers to feel complete.

This is where I stop asking, Where do I belong?
and start knowing—I am already there.
Home is no longer a place I wait to be welcomed into,
or a person I hope will choose me.
Home is the space I've built within myself,
the one I carry wherever I go.

The poems in this section are not about arrival in someone else's arms—
though love is still here, steady and present.
They are about the deeper arrival:
the moment I recognized that the peace I'd been chasing
had been waiting inside me all along.

Here, love is no longer survival or longing or even proof.
It is a companion to my wholeness,
a reflection of the truth I already know:
I am mine.
Fully.
And I am enough.

If the earlier sections were about healing, living, and standing whole,
this is about dwelling—secure, unshaken, and free—
in the life I've claimed for myself.

This is the closing chapter.
The place where my story no longer begins with someone else's name.
Because home—
after all this time—
is my own.

—L.S.

Letter to the Reader: "Becoming Mine"

If The Spark and the Surrender was about falling in love, and The Silence Between was about learning to endure distance, then Becoming Mine—both the book and this poem—is about something far more intimate: returning to myself.

For far too long, I, like many women, was taught that my body was utilitarian. It was a vessel—for service, for sacrifice, for survival. It carried children, it carried burdens, it carried others. But it rarely carried *me*. And so, without bitterness or resentment, I moved through the world in this body without ever truly possessing it.

The original poem, titled *My Body*, emerged during a time of profound self-discovery. I was approaching forty, a milestone often associated with wisdom and reflection. For the first time, I began to view my body not as an object to be given away, not as a tool of production or performance, but as something *mine*—something sacred, sensual, and deeply worthy of attention, tenderness, and joy.

This poem honors that shift. It honors the gentle return to self. The unraveling of beliefs that told me my body belonged more to others than it ever did to me. And yes, it also honors love—the kind of love that doesn't demand possession, but offers permission. The kind of intimacy that gently teaches you how to look in the mirror and say, *"This body is mine. And I love her."*

If you have ever felt disconnected from your own reflection, if you've ever struggled to feel pleasure that wasn't about someone else's satisfaction, I hope this poem speaks to you. May it offer a reminder: that your body is yours. Entirely. Gloriously. Beautifully. Yours.

With compassion and courage,

–L.S.

Becoming Mine

formerly titled "My Body"

I have never hated my body,
nor longed for another's.
I am not angry with the afflictions
that dwell in my bones and blood.
I understand this body—
its disorder, its rhythm—
and how to live my best life in it,
without complaint.

Still, for much of my life,
I did not take pleasure in it.
I saw my body as a tool—
a carrier of burdens:
children, products, expectations.
It was used to serve,
to satisfy others,
rarely, if ever, myself.

I never stood before a mirror
and delighted in what I saw.
Never inhaled my own scent
with desire.
Never touched my skin
to spark my own satisfaction.

Not because I hated it—
but because I was taught
that my body was not mine.
Not wholly.

After my first child,
my doctor told me,
"Your breasts are no longer just for pleasure."
He was not wrong.
They became a supply line,
a source of life.
For years,
arousal was silenced.
Touch lost its meaning.
And no one warned me
how long it would take to return.

Now,
I approach forty
with new eyes,
new hands,
a new mind.

It is liberating
to finally embrace my body
for my joy.
No longer just a vessel—
but a sanctuary.
No longer just a service—
but a source of celebration.

I love to touch,
to smell,
to taste,
to know myself—
not out of necessity,
but desire.

I love sharing this body with you.
Through your presence,
your patience,
your passion—
I've discovered new corners of myself.

With you,
my body speaks.
With you,
my body learns.
And each day,
forty grows sweeter.

Thank you—
for being part of the return.

Your guidance.
Your support.
Your unwavering encouragement.

They've given me permission
not only to explore you,
but to finally
come home
to me.

Letter to the Reader: "The Love of Her Own Life"

"The Love of Her Own Life" is a declaration—a reminder of a woman's power to rebuild, to rise, and to reclaim her own reflection after being defined for too long by the world around her. It was written from a place of both strength and honesty, born of lived experiences that taught me the difference between surviving for others and truly living for myself.

The poem speaks to the resilience of women who have learned to stand again after being broken, who have carried both love and loss, and who finally understand that choosing themselves is not abandonment—it is preservation. The "bricks others have thrown" represent the criticism, rejection, and betrayal that life often delivers, sometimes from those closest to us. A strong woman learns not to throw those bricks back, but to use them as building blocks—a foundation for her peace, her independence, and her rebirth.

The image of being "thrown to a pack of wolves" yet returning as the leader of the pack captures the transformation that happens when pain becomes purpose. Strength is not simply survival—it's evolution. She learns to navigate her own wilderness, to hunt for her own wholeness, and to feed herself the validation she once sought from others.

Yet, beneath her strength lies tenderness. The poem acknowledges that she does not leave because she stops loving; she leaves because staying would mean losing herself. That distinction is powerful. It reminds us that self-love is not selfish—it's sacred. It's the act of ensuring that our hearts continue to beat in alignment with who we are becoming.

At its heart, *"The Love of Her Own Life"* celebrates the moment a woman realizes that her worth does not depend on another's affection. She does not choose loneliness; she chooses authenticity. She learns to pour love into her own soul until someone equally whole arrives—not to complete her, but to complement her.

As you read this poem, I hope you see not just a story of independence, but a reflection of your own capacity to begin again. To build. To lead. To love yourself first and best. Because every woman deserves to be her own safe place, her own healing, and yes— her own great love.

With strength and light,

—L.S.

The Love of Her Own Life

A strong woman
builds her foundation
from the very bricks
meant to break her.
What was hurled in hate,
she stacks in strength—
stone by stone,
lesson by lesson.

When cast to the wolves,
she doesn't run.
She rises,
teeth bared not in fear,
but in command.
She leads the pack,
not because she was born to,
but because she chose to survive
when others expected her to fall.

She hunts with precision,
brings home the kill,
nourishes with power
carved from persistence.

And when she walks away,
don't mistake it for lack of love.
She leaves not because
her love ran dry,
but because the longer she stayed,
the further she drifted

from the woman
she fought so hard to become.

She doesn't want to be alone.
She simply knows
that loving herself
is not optional—
it's essential.

Until someone comes
worthy enough
to stand beside her,
to match her peace
and mirror her purpose,
she'll remain
the love
of her own life.

Closing Letter to the Reader

Dear Reader,

When I began The Spark and the Surrender, I didn't set out to write a trilogy. I only knew that my heart was overflowing with something too alive, too real, to keep to myself. That first book was pure spring—newness everywhere, possibility in every glance, every word, every breath. It was a season of awakening, of learning what it feels like to be chosen, pursued, and seen in ways I had only imagined. The pages danced with joy and wonder, with the fresh fire of love at first bloom.

Then came The Silence Between—and with it, the shift. Summer's heat gave way to the slower, cooler winds of autumn. Here, the story turned inward. The poems grew heavier in places, softer in others, holding the weight of questions that didn't yet have answers. This season carried the ache of distance, the stretching of patience, and the quiet work of tending love when it was no longer new, but still worth keeping. It was a time of reckoning—learning that love can endure, but it must also adapt.

And now, Becoming Mine—the winter that bends back toward spring. These are the poems of reclamation, of realizing that wholeness does not come from another person's presence alone, but from the life and spirit God placed in me from the beginning. It is about the courage to keep loving without losing myself, the discipline of holding space for another while also honoring the space I need for my own growth. It is about embracing love not as my foundation, but as a home I choose to visit—while remembering that my truest home is in God, in my own spirit, in the woman I've fought to become.

Across these three books, I have invited you into my seasons. Together, we've stood in the spark of something new, waited in the ache of uncertainty, and arrived in the quiet power of self-possession. But I must tell you—the story isn't over. I have written hundreds of poems that trace this relationship through its joys, complexities, silences, and resurgences. There are chapters still unopened, letters still sealed, moments still waiting to find their way to you.

If you carry anything from this trilogy, let it be this: It is possible to live your truth while staying grounded in your faith. To be both deeply in love and deeply rooted in God. To remain firm in your convictions, even when the world tells you to bend. To trust that the One who is in control of all things—all narratives, all timelines—knows how to weave every piece of your story into something whole and good.

We are all in the process of becoming—becoming stronger, becoming softer, becoming more of who we were meant to be. And sometimes, love is part of that becoming. Sometimes, it is the mirror that shows us what's already within. And sometimes, it is the lesson that reminds us we belong fully to ourselves and to God before we belong to anyone else.

Thank you for walking with me through these pages, for reading not just my poems but my heart. Thank you for allowing these books to be both personal and shared, intimate and universal. Thank you for finding pieces of your own story here, and for letting them speak to the truth of your own becoming.

This is farewell for now, not forever. There will be more. More words, more seasons, more truths offered in love. And when they arrive, I hope you meet them with the same openness and grace you've given these pages.

Until then, live fully. Love deeply. Stand firmly in your truth. And trust the Author who holds the pen to every story—yours, mine, and all the ones we have yet to tell.

The pen is still moving.
The story is still unfolding.
And I promise—
there is more to come.

With all my heart,

Lueella Shelton

Benediction

May you carry your truth

like light in your hands,

steady and unshaken.

May love find you

and keep you soft,

but never smaller.

And may you remember—

the Author of your story

is still writing,

and the best chapters

are yet to come.

—Lueella Shelton

Epilogue

There are love stories that unfold all at once—fast, bright, and complete in a single breath. And then, there are those that arrive in seasons. Sixteen of them, to be exact. Each one with its own weather, its own lesson, its own way of teaching the heart what it means to stay, to change, to surrender, and to rise again.

Becoming Mine was never about ownership—it was about arrival. The arrival of self after breaking open. The arrival of love after loss. The arrival of truth after silence. Each poem in these pages has traced the journey of what it means to become—through desire, through reflection, through the gentle undoing of everything you once thought love required.

But this is not where the story ends. The next collection carries us deeper, into the full circle of *sixteen seasons.* It is there that every storm, every sunrise, every moment of distance and return will be named. From the first spark of discovery to the final quiet of devotion, these seasons reveal not just two lovers bound by time, but two souls learning how to breathe within it.

The new work will not shy away from the weight of truth—the misunderstandings, the pauses, the reconciliations that define real connection. It will honor the way love grows not only in its brightest hours, but in the long, gray seasons where growth hides beneath the surface. It will remember that passion can be holy, that patience is its own kind of intimacy, and that freedom does not end where love begins.

When the next book opens, it will no longer be about *becoming mine—*
but *becoming ours.*

Sixteen seasons.
One story.
Told through the language of time,
and the poetry of love that refused to fade.

— Lueella Shelton

About the Author

Lueella Shelton is an author, poet, educator, and historian whose work blends unflinching honesty with tender intimacy. Her writing captures the complexity of love, the necessity of self-discovery, and the quiet strength of living in one's truth.

She is the founder of Shelton Legacy Press, LLC, a publishing company dedicated to helping authors bring their stories to life while honoring their unique voices. Drawing on her background in education and historical preservation, Lueella approaches storytelling as both art and testimony—carefully crafted, deeply felt, and grounded in lived experience.

Becoming Mine is the third volume in her Ink to Paper trilogy, following The Spark and the Surrender and The Silence Between. Across these three books, she invites readers into the seasons of a love story—its passion, its pauses, and its transformations—while charting her own journey toward self-possession and faith-filled resilience.

Her poetry often bridges the personal and the universal, offering readers not only a glimpse into her own life, but a mirror for their own joys, struggles, and becoming. With hundreds of poems still unreleased, she continues to document love, healing, and the pursuit of wholeness in all its forms.

Lueella lives and writes in Texas, where she finds inspiration in quiet mornings, meaningful conversations, and the enduring belief that the best stories—like the best love—are written with both courage and grace.

You can connect with her at www.lulu-writes.com to follow her work, discover upcoming releases, and share your own stories of love, faith, and becoming.

*If The Spark and the Surrender was the falling,
and The Silence Between was the waiting—
then Becoming Mine is the standing.*

In the final volume of the Ink to Paper trilogy, Lueella Shelton brings readers into the season of return—not just to love, but to herself. These poems trace the slow, radical unfolding that happens when a woman stops chasing clarity in someone else's eyes and begins finding it in her own reflection.

Here are letters of peace and power. Of memory and mourning. Of love that endures without clinging, and selfhood that stands without apology. Through intimate verse and unguarded confession, Shelton explores what it means to be whole—even still—after longing, after healing, after becoming.

Becoming Mine is not a breakup collection. It is a becoming collection. It is a testimony to the truth that you can love deeply without losing yourself, live your truth while staying grounded in faith, and remain firm in your convictions knowing that the Author of all stories is still writing yours.

With hundreds of poems still to come, this is not the end—it is simply the close of one chapter, and the promise of another.

www.ingramcontent.com/pod-product-compliance
Lightning Source LLC
Chambersburg PA
CBHW051700090426
42736CB00013B/2457